GUMMY FUN

Chewy Treats for the Whole Family

Hisako Ogita

VERTICAL.

CONTENTS

PART 1 Juice Gummies

Fruit Juice Gummies

Fruit and Veggie Variations

Japanese Milk-Based Drink Gummies

Dairy Drinks

Store-Bought Drinks

PART 2 Purée Gummies

Fruit Purée Gummies

Various Purées

Fruit Purée

Ready-Made Purées

Canned Fruit

PART 3 Tea and Coffee Gummies

Green Tea Gummies

Various Kinds of Tea

Herb Tea Gummies

Coffee and Black Tea

gummy boy   gummy girl

gummy starlets

gummy-lover
Megumi

【 Notes on measurements 】

◎ The original metric measurements are listed first with US equivalents in parentheses. Converted measurements vary in format to keep the measurements as close to common usage as possible. For the most reliable results, use a kitchen scale and work with the metric measurements. Keep in mind that 1 ml = 1 g.

◎ In this book: 1 C = 250 ml, 1 Tbsp = 15 ml, 1 tsp = 5 ml.

◎ Final gummy volume is not given. Err on the generous side when working with more concentrated liquids in the recipes. Cooking times for simmered ingredients will vary depending on the size and thickness of the pan. Use the listed cooking times as guidelines, not absolutes.

◎ Please use caution when giving gummies to young children or the elderly, as they may choke. Please cut into small pieces or monitor chewing.

◎ Hand-made gummies will not stay fresh for more than a few days. Carefully wrap up any leftovers and consume within 2 to 3 days of making.

Make all kinds of yummy
gummy treats on your own.

Just use whatever
ingredients you have
on hand!

6

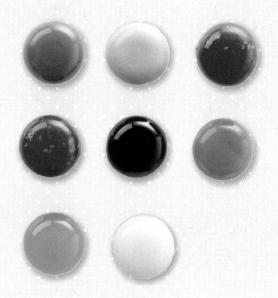

Try using juice,

Upsie!!

or purées or canned foods,

or coffee
or tea,

or even liqueur
or syrup.

A B C D E F G
H I J K L M N
O P Q R S T U
V W X Y Z

Amazing! So delicious!

Tools you need to make your own gummies

It's easy to make gummies. You don't need many tools,
but depending on the ingredients you might need more than what I list here.
These are the basics, aside from gummy molds.

1. Pan: Used for flat, even gummies.

2. Tea strainer: Used to strain tea leaves from tea. The finer the mesh the better.

3. Measuring spoons: Deep-set spoons are easier to use.

4. Spoon: Used to ladle gummy liquid into molds.

5. Juicer: Used to squeeze fresh juice from fruit.

6. Grater: Used to zest lemons, grate carrots, etc.

7. Kitchen scale: The gummy recipes call for small amounts of ingredients, and a scale helps ensure correct proportions. Use both ml measuring spoons and the scale (1 ml = 1 g) for liquid ingredients.

8. Measuring cup: Used for liquid measurements. Check exactly from the side.

9. Rubber/silicone spatula: Used for stirring hot liquids, so pick one that's heat-safe.

10. Pot: The volume for gummies is small, so use a small pot or pan made from stainless steel.

11. Bowls: Used to combine ingredients. I recommend stainless steel, which transmits heat.

12. Electric food mill: Used to purée ingredients. A small one is fine. Or use a mixer.

Basic ingredients for gummies

There are many different ingredients that can be used for gummies. This is an introduction to the most commonly used.

1. Sheet gelatin: Gelatin that has been rolled into sheets and dried. Use only cold water to soften.

2. Powdered gelatin: May come as a powder or small granules. Always add powdered gelatin to liquid, not the other way around.

3. Powdered *kanten* (Japanese agar): A gelling agent made from seaweed. It's difficult to melt, so stir constantly over heat for two minutes to dissolve.

4. Skim milk: Used for milk-flavored gummies.

5. Lemon juice: Add to gummies to cut sweetness. Always use in pectin-based recipes to bring out firmness.

6. Pectin: Most commonly used as a gelling agent in jam and jelly. Pectin gives a stickier texture and consistency than gelatin.

7. Agar: A gelling agent made from seaweed. Combine with sugar, then add to liquid. Bring to a boil to dissolve. Agar gives a springier texture than gelatin.

8. Granulated sugar: Used as a sweetener. Slightly less sweet than an equal amount of powdered sugar (which is also OK to use).

9. Corn syrup: Yields tacky gummies. Also acts as a preservative.

All kinds of molds

It will be hard to find molds sold specifically for gummies, so use chocolate molds or special ice cube trays or other such molds. Making gummies is even more fun if you have a variety of molds to choose from, so work on slowly building up your collection.

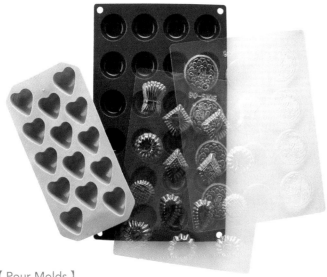

【 Pour Molds 】

Molds are generally made of plastic or silicone. Make sure of how much heat the molds can tolerate. Most of the gummy liquids will be around 140°F (60°C) when poured into molds, so make sure the molds are designed for such temperatures. Gummies can be tricky to remove from plastic molds, so try spraying with cooking spray before pouring in gummy liquid to make them easier to remove.

Tricks for getting gummies out of molds
Remove gummies as soon as they've set up.

For plastic molds
Press the gummy down gently with a fingertip as you pull back the mold. Be careful to avoid crushing the gummy.

For silicone molds
Since the material is soft, press the gummy up and out from the back of the mold. Silicone molds are easier to use than plastic, but the shapes tend to be more limited.

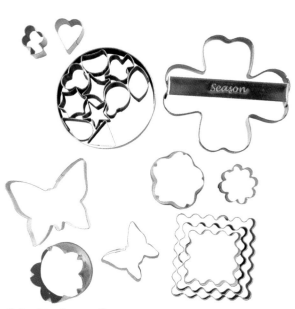

【Cookie Cutters】

Used to cut cookie dough or vegetables into different shapes.
These won't create a pattern on the surface of the gummies, but
they're great for creating clean shapes. Pour the gummy liquid into
the mold evenly for neat, pretty gummies.

Tricks for using cutters

1. Line a flat-bottomed container with plastic wrap.
Pour in gummy liquid. Storage containers or
shallow pans are easy to use.
2. Once the liquid has gelled, remove wrap along
with gummy, place on work surface and cut out
using cutters.

How to work with gelatin—the star ingredient in gummies

Gelatin is the ingredient that gives gummies their chewy texture. Gelatin is a gelling agent comprised mainly of the collagen (protein) from the hooves and skin of cows or pigs. Here I'll introduce different kinds of gelatin as well as other types of gelling agents.

There's a variety of gelatins to choose from

Gelatin comes in a variety of forms, from the small bags in the grocery store to the large containers used by professional cooks. Gelatin comes in powdered or sheet form. The sheets yield a more translucent finished product. The powdered form comes in two types: one that's "bloomed" in water before use, and another that's directly added to other ingredients. The same amount of gelatin from different manufacturers can yield different results, so test out various kinds until you get the knack of working with them. Cooking gelatin with lemon juice or other highly acidic ingredients will keep gelatin from easily setting up. Also, ingredients with protease (enzymes that break down protein) such as raw pineapples, papayas, mangoes or figs will break down gelatin, so they can't be used in gelatin-based recipes. If you want to use such ingredients, cook them first, as heat breaks down the enzymes.

How to use gelatin

1

2

A

Powdered gelatin

For bloomed types: Add into indicated amount of water (ph. 1), stir (ph. 2) and let it absorb water. Dissolve in 100-120°F (40-50°C) liquid. For direct-use types: Dissolve in 100-120°F (40-50°C) liquid (ph. A). In either case, remove pan from heat and let liquid cool before adding gelatin.

Sheet gelatin

Roll up gelatin sheet and submerge in ice water. Thin sheets need 5 minutes to soak; thicker sheets need about 10. Place in refrigerator during summer months or if you won't be using the gelatin right away. Once reconstituted, press out excess water. Heat liquid in pan, remove from heat and add gelatin and stir until dissolved.

Add agar or pectin for a wide range of textures

Agar

Agar is a gelling agent derived from red algae. It's appealing because it solidifies at room temperature and has a higher melting point than gelatin. Combining agar with gelatin yields a springier texture.

Pectin

Pectin is a gelling agent mainly found in citrus fruit rinds or apple pomace. Combining pectin with gelatin yields a stickier texture.

17

Introduction

Gummies have uniquely squishy, springy and sticky textures. Gummies are traditionally seen in the West, but recently they've become popular in Japan, too.

Gummies are appealing because their texture is somewhere between the softness of jelly and the firmness of licorice and also because they come in an array of colors, fragrances and shapes. Kids and grown-ups alike love gummies. Being able to make your own gummies expands the horizons of your treat-making abilities. Plus, if you make them yourself you know there are no chemical additives, so you can enjoy them with peace of mind. Doesn't that make it worth it?

In this book I'll introduce recipes that feature juice, purée and tea-based gummies with soft textures. Let's make gummies in all kinds of shapes, from all kinds of ingredients, in a wide variety of colors and flavors. The instructions are very simple, so try making them with your kids. They make perfect gifts and are welcome at parties, too.

Home-made gummies are different from store-bought ones. Try out just one recipe. Before long you'll want to make more and more.
I sincerely hope the circle of gummy-lovers keeps expanding.

Hisako Ogita

Juice Gummies

Hand-pressed fruit juice is fresh both in fragrance and flavor.

Boil down the fruit juice to concentrate. Fruit gummies are small but packed with goodness. Enjoy the fresh fruit flavors that only hand-made gummies can give.

Fruit Juice Gummies

Citrus fruits have citric acid which cuts down sweetness, making it perfect for gummies. The final volume should be the amount of concentrated juice plus 10 g (1/3 oz). So use 50 g (1 3/4 oz) concentrate for approximately 60 g (2 oz) yield.

【 Basic instructions 】
Orange

1

Slice orange in half and squeeze onto juicer.

2

Add 100 ml (2/5 C) juice to a small pan and heat over low.

3

Simmer over low heat until reduced to 50 ml (1/5 C).
Use a scale to ensure you have 50 g.

4

Add water to a small bowl.
Add powdered gelatin and bloom (3 to 5 minutes).

【 Ingredients 】

100 ml (2/5 C) juice of 1 orange

10 g (1/3 oz) powdered gelatin

1 Tbsp water

15 g (3 2/3 tsp) granulated sugar

1 tsp lemon juice

1 tsp corn syrup

5

Add sugar, lemon juice and corn syrup to pan. Raise heat to medium.

6

Stir with a rubber spatula until sugar and syrup are dissolved.

7

Once at a gentle boil, turn off heat. Add gelatin and stir slowly with spatula, taking care to avoid adding bubbles.

8

Once gelatin is totally dissolved, pour liquid into molds and let set at room temperature.

Fruit and Veggie Variations

There's a whole range of options aside from oranges. Here is a recipe for lemon, but try grapefruit or other citrus flavors, too. Veggie versions like carrot and tomato are full of vitamins, making them very healthy treats.

Lemon

〖 Ingredients 〗
Zest of 1/2 lemon
25 ml (1 2/3 Tbsp) fresh-squeezed lemon juice (1 lemon)
30 g (2 1/2 Tbsp) granulated sugar
10 g (1/3 oz) powdered gelatin
2 Tbsp water
1 tsp corn syrup

〖 Instructions 〗
Zest yellow part of lemon rind (ph. 1) and squeeze out and keep juice. Combine 1 tsp sugar and rub on a cutting board and muddle (ph. 2). Follow steps 4 through 8 of the recipe for orange gummies (p. 20-21). In step 5, add lemon juice, muddled sugar and zest, remaining sugar and 1 Tbsp water and heat over medium.

Carrot

〖 Ingredients 〗
50 ml (1/5 C) carrot juice
10 g (1/3 oz) powdered gelatin
1 Tbsp water
20 g (1 2/3 Tbsp) granulated sugar
1 tsp lemon juice
1 tsp corn syrup

〖 Instructions 〗
Follow basic instructions for orange gummies (p. 20-21). For steps 1 through 3, grate carrots (ph. 1) and press out liquid with strainer (ph. 2) until you have 50 ml (2/5 C) juice. Add juice in step 5. The rest is the same.

Cherry Tomato

〖 Ingredients 〗
100 g (3 1/2 oz) cherry tomatoes
15 g (1/2 oz) powdered gelatin
2 Tbsp water
20 g (1 2/3 Tbsp) granulated sugar
1 tsp lemon juice
1 tsp corn syrup

〖 Instructions 〗
Follow basic instructions for orange gummies (p. 20-21). For steps 1 through 3, remove stems from tomatoes, blanch (ph. 1), immediately place in cold water, remove skins and chop (ph. 2). Add to a small pan and heat over low until reduced to 50 g (1/5 C). In step 4, bloom gelatin in 2 Tbsp water. Add liquid to pan in step 5. The rest is the same.

LEMON

CHERRY TOMATO

ORANGE

CARROT

Japanese Milk-Based Drink Gummies

Gummies work best with liquid bases that are concentrated in flavor. Calpico and Yakult already come in concentrated form, making them very convenient to use. These items can be found in Asian grocery stores. Try making gummies from other commercially available juices and drinks, concentrating them down to a fifth.

【 Dairy Drinks 】

Since these already come in concentrated form, there's no need to take the step of reducing the liquid.
You can whip these gummies up even faster than other kinds.

 ### Calpico

【 Ingredients 】
50 ml (1/5 C) + 1 Tbsp Calpico
10 g (1/3 oz) powdered gelatin
1 tsp lemon juice
1 tsp corn syrup

【 Instructions 】
Add 1 Tbsp Calpico to a bowl. Add gelatin and let sit for 3 to 5 minutes (ph.). Add remaining Calpico, lemon juice and corn syrup to a small pan and heat over medium while stirring with a rubber spatula. Once at a gentle boil, turn off heat. Add gelatin and stir slowly with spatula, taking care to avoid adding bubbles. Once gelatin is totally dissolved, pour liquid into molds and let set at room temperature.

 ### Yakult

【 Ingredients 】
50 ml (1 2/3 oz (1/5 C)) + 1Tbsp
　Yakult (yogurt drink)
10 g (1/3 oz) powdered gelatin
1 tsp corn syrup

【 Instructions 】
Add 1 Tbsp Yakult to a bowl. Add gelatin and let sit for 3 to 5 minutes. Add remaining Yakult and corn syrup to a small pan and heat over medium while stirring with a rubber spatula. Once at a gentle boil, turn off heat. Add gelatin and stir slowly with spatula, taking care to avoid adding bubbles. Once gelatin is totally dissolved, pour liquid into molds and let set at room temperature.

YAKULT

CALPICO

【 Store-Bought Drinks 】

These gummies are prepared the same way as the other juice gummies, only there's no need to squeeze the fruit yourself. Also, reconstitute the gelatin directly in the drink liquid, not water.

Try making gummies out of your favorite beverages.

Grape

Grapefruit

Acerola

Orange

Cola

【 Ingredients 】

250 ml (1 C) juice/soda/drink

5 g (1 1/4 tsp) granulated sugar

10 g (1/3 oz) powdered gelatin

1 tsp lemon juice*

1 tsp corn syrup

*Don't use lemon juice with acerola juice.

【 Instructions 】

Follow basic instructions for orange gummies (p. 20-21). For steps 1 through 3, reserve 1 Tbsp of juice and add the rest to a small pan and heat over low (ph.) until reduced to 50 ml (1/5 C). In step 4, bloom gelatin in 1 Tbsp juice. The rest is the same.

When you reduce store-bought beverages, they end up looking like this.

Boil 235 ml for 20 minutes to yield 50 ml liquid.

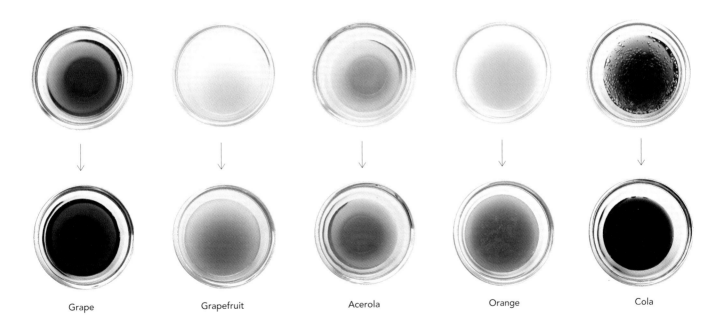

Grape Grapefruit Acerola Orange Cola

GRAPE

ACEROLA

ORANGE

GRAPEFRUIT

JUICE

COLA

Polka-Dot Gummies

This is a super easy way to make gummies without molds.
Simply drop dots of gummy liquid onto a work surface with a spoon.
Using just one type of gummy lets you create a cute polka-dot pattern,
but add another for a colorful variation. Draw shapes with the liquid
on a plate or tray, let set, then peel off and eat.
This is a great way to make snack time even more exciting.

The original German gummi

Gummies, spelled "gummi" in German (meaning "rubber"), refer to gummy candies. The first gummy candy was invented by Hans Riegel in the 1920's in Bonn, Germany, in response to reports that children's chewing capabilities were weakening and tooth disease was on the rise. His gummies were on the tougher side, made from fruit juice, gelatin and corn starch. Riegel founded the now-famous candy company Haribo. Made with an emphasis on texture, the first gummy recipes called for 30-40% gelatin.

Nowadays you can find gummy candies in groceries and convenience stores in any country. They're popular among kids and adults, men and women. The gelatin-based ones have collagen in them, which keeps your skin supple, making them a popular choice for the beauty-minded.

The gummies of Germany tend to be tougher, while soft gummies are more popular in Japan. In this book, I focus on softer types of gummies.

Purée Gummies

Gummies made from fruit purées have the unique, toothsome texture of fiber, making them even more fruity. Try whipping up your own purées with a mill or mixer or buy commercially available purées. Enjoy the world of fruity gummies.

Fruit Purée Gummies

It's best to use fruits that are in season, but ready-made purées are handy year-round. The finished gummies are always colorful. If you're using frozen purée, use a fork to scoop out the amount the recipe calls for.

〖 Basic instructions 〗
Strawberry Purée

1

Rinse strawberries and remove stems. Purée with a mill or mixer.

2

Pour 60 ml (appx. 1/4 C) into a measuring cup. Use a scale to ensure you have 60 g.

3

Add water to a small bowl. Add powdered gelatin and bloom (3 to 5 minutes).

4

Combine sugar and pectin.

【 Ingredients 】
70 g (2 1/2 oz) strawberries
8 g (1/4 oz) powdered gelatin
1 Tbsp water
30 g (2 1/2 Tbsp) granulated sugar
5 g (1/8 oz) dry pectin
1 tsp lemon juice
1 tsp corn syrup

5

Add puréed strawberries and then sugar and pectin to a small pan.

6

Heat over medium-low. Stir in lemon juice and corn syrup. Once at a gentle boil, turn heat to low, simmer for 2 minutes and stir.

7

Turn off heat. Add bloomed gelatin and stir with a rubber spatula, taking care to avoid adding bubbles.

8

Once gelatin is totally dissolved, pour liquid into molds and let set at room temperature.

Various Purées

You can use puréed fresh fruit or store-bought purée, frozen or canned. Any kind of puréed fruit will result in refreshingly sweet and tangy gummies. Try using all kinds of molds for a whole range of gummies.

【 Fruit Purée 】

These recipes follow the same basic instructions for the Strawberry Purée gummies (p. 32-33), but the amount of purée and sugar varies depending on the fruit used. I made these using a simple round silicone mold.

Kiwi

【 Ingredients 】
60 g (just over 2 oz) kiwi
8 g (1/4 oz) powdered gelatin
1 Tbsp water
30 g (2 1/2 Tbsp) granulated sugar
5 g (1/8 oz) dry pectin
1 tsp lemon juice
1 tsp corn syrup

【 Instructions 】
Follow basic instructions for strawberry purée gummies (p. 32-33). For steps 1 and 2, unpeel and purée kiwi in a mill or mixer. Make sure you end up with 50 ml (1 3/4 oz). The rest is the same.

Blueberry

【 Ingredients 】
50 g (1/3 C) blueberries
40 g (3 1/4 Tbsp) granulated sugar
8 g (1/4 oz) powdered gelatin
2 Tbsp water
5 g (1/8 oz) dry pectin
1 tsp lemon juice
1 tsp corn syrup

【 Instructions 】
Follow basic instructions for strawberry purée gummies (p. 32-33). For steps 1 and 2, purée blueberries in a mill or mixer. Make sure you end up with 40 ml (1 1/2 oz). Combine with 1 Tbsp water, then strain. The rest is the same.

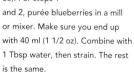

Melon

【 Ingredients 】
70 g (2 1/2 oz) melon
8 g (1/4 oz) powdered gelatin
1 Tbsp water
30 g (2 1/2 Tbsp) granulated sugar
5 g (1/8 oz) dry pectin
1 tsp lemon juice
1 tsp corn syrup

【 Instructions 】
Follow basic instructions for strawberry purée gummies (p. 32-33). For steps 1 and 2, remove rind and seeds from melon and purée in a mill or mixer. Make sure you end up with 50 ml (1 3/4 oz). The rest is the same.

Raspberry

【 Ingredients 】
60 g (1/2 C) raspberries
8 g (1/4 oz) powdered gelatin
1 Tbsp water
30 g (2 1/2 Tbsp) granulated sugar
5 g (1/8 oz) dry pectin
1 tsp lemon juice
1 tsp corn syrup

【 Instructions 】
Follow basic instructions for strawberry purée gummies (p. 32-33). For steps 1 and 2, purée raspberries in a mill or mixer. Make sure you end up with 50 ml (1 3/4 oz). The rest is the same.

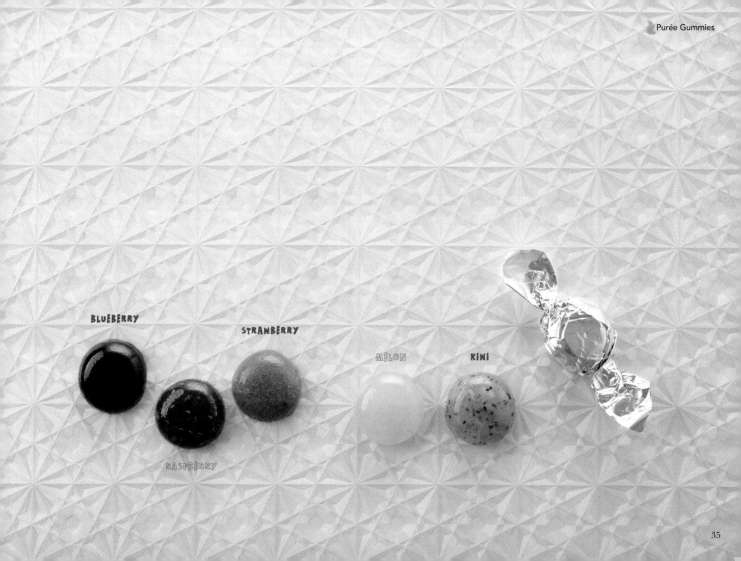

BLUEBERRY

STRANBERRY

MÉLON

KIWI

RASPBERRY

【 Ready-Made Purées 】

Since these ingredients come already puréed, they're super easy to use. I poured the gummy liquid into a pan and used cookie cutters to create individual gummies. Cookie cutters are easier to use than molds, a great advantage.

Apricot Purée

Mango Purée

Green Apple Purée

Cassis Purée

Pink Peach Purée

【 Ingredients 】

50 g (1 3/4 oz) purée
10 g (1/3 oz) powdered gelatin
1 Tbsp water
10 g (2 1/2 tsp) granulated sugar
5 g (1/8 oz) dry pectin
1 tsp lemon juice
2 tsp corn syrup

【 Instructions 】

Follow basic instructions for strawberry purée gummies (p. 32-33). For steps 1 and 2, simply use the purée of your choice. In step 8, line a pan with plastic wrap and pour in gummy liquid (ph.). Once set up, pull out of pan along with plastic wrap and cut out with cookie cutters.

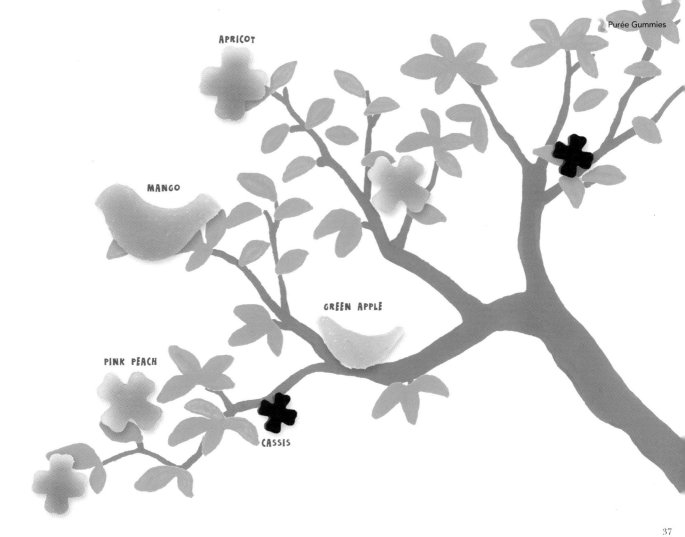

APRICOT

MANGO

GREEN APPLE

PINK PEACH

CASSIS

【 Canned Fruit 】

Canned stuff are cheap and always on grocery shelves, which is very convenient.
Pineapples have protease, an enzyme that breaks down gelatin's protein, so it can't be used raw in gummies, but canned pineapple has been cooked and works for gummy recipes.

White Peach

Pineapple

Yellow Peach

【 Ingredients 】

70 g (1/3 C) canned fruit, drained
15 g (1/2 oz) powdered gelatin
2 Tbsp water
10 g (2 1/2 tsp) granulated sugar
5 g (1/8 oz) dry pectin
1 tsp lemon juice
1 tsp corn syrup

【 Instructions 】

Follow basic instructions
for strawberry purée
gummies (p. 32-33).
Purée drained canned
fruits. Bloom gelatin in
water (ph.).

WHITE PEACH

PINEAPPLE

YELLOW PEACH

Rope Gummies

These don't need any molds. Spread out an even layer of gummy liquid, let set up, then slice into 1/2" strips. Tie the strips into knots to make gummy pretzels. These are really easy to make, so try it out.

Depression Mold Gummies

Layer corn starch inside a pan. Use the bottom of a glass or wooden blocks to create depressions in the starch. Pour gummy liquid into the molds. If the liquid is too hot it'll melt the starch, so be sure to let it cool slightly before pouring. Once set up, use a brush to dust off starch. The surface will be smooth and non-tacky, making these easy to handle.
Use whatever you have on hand to create the molds.

Fondue Gummies

Simply skewer a piece of fruit and dredge through gummy liquid. The fruit ends up shiny in a gummy glaze and very tasty-looking. It looks like jelly, but the texture is a surprising combination of springy gummy and juicy fruit. These are perfect for kids' snacks or dessert.

Tea and Coffee Gummies

You can make gummies with tea or coffee.

The trick is to use strong brews.

If you carry some soothing tea in gummy form,

you can have a little tea time wherever you want.

Green Tea Gummies

Try making gummies with Japan's flagship beverage—green tea.

For this recipe, don't use hot water. Use room temperature water and steep for a long time.

This technique yields much nicer-looking gummies.

But if you don't have time, hot water-steeped tea will work just fine.

Use powdered gelatin that doesn't need to be bloomed.

【 Basic instructions 】

Green Tea

【 Ingredients 】

10 g (1/3 oz) green tea leaves

100 ml (2/5 C) water

10 g (2 1/2 tsp) granulated sugar

1 tsp corn syrup

10 g (1/3 oz) powdered gelatin

1

Combine tea and water. Steep in refrigerator for 2 to 3 hours.

2

Once strong enough, strain out tea leaves.

3

Pour 50 ml (1/5 C) into a measuring cup. Use a scale to ensure you have 50 g.

4

Combine green tea, sugar and corn syrup in a small pan and heat over medium.

5

Once the sugar has melted and the mixture is gently boiling, turn off heat.

6

Gradually stir in gelatin.

7

Once gelatin is totally dissolved, pour liquid into molds and let set at room temperature.

Various Kinds of Tea

Try making gummies with other kinds of tea such as fragrant roasted *houji* tea or vivid powdered *maccha* tea.
Use gelatin that doesn't need to be bloomed first.
Pop a catechin-filled tea gummy in your mouth for an instant pick-me-up.

Roasted Tea (*houji cha*)

[Ingredients]
10 g (1/3 oz) roasted tea leaves
80 ml (1/3 C) hot water
10 g (2 1/2 tsp) granulated sugar
1 tsp corn syrup
10 g (1/3 oz) powdered gelatin

[Instructions]
Follow basic instructions
for Green Tea gummies
(p. 44-45). Brew strong
roasted tea and measure
out 50 ml (1/5 C).

Powdered Green Tea (*maccha*)

[Ingredients]
5 g (2 1/2 tsp) powdered green tea (*maccha*)
50 ml (1/5 C) hot water
20 g (1 2/3 Tbsp) granulated sugar
1 tsp corn syrup
10 g (1/3 oz) powdered gelatin

[Instructions]
Follow basic instructions for
Green Tea gummies (p. 44-
45). Add powdered green
tea to a small bowl and
gradually stir in hot water.

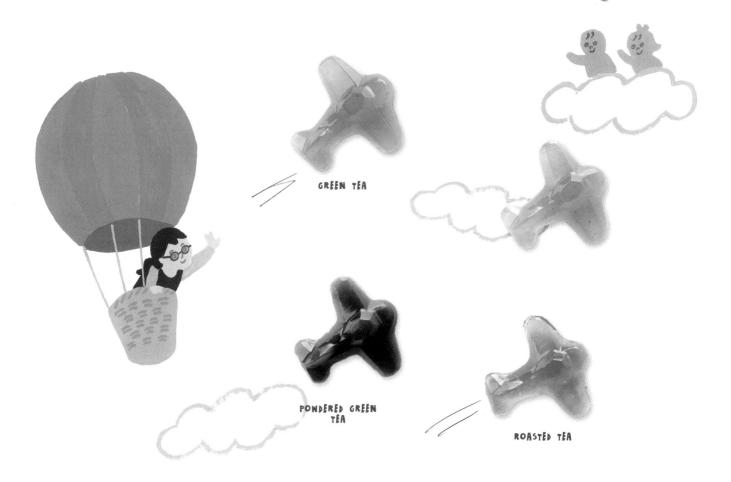

GREEN TEA

POWDERED GREEN TEA

ROASTED TEA

Herb Tea Gummies

The invigorating, menthol flavor of peppermint. The vivid, tangy taste of hibiscus.
Adding fresh mint leaves allows a cool flavor to take over your taste buds.
Herbs have all kinds of health benefits so these gummies are great for you.

Mint Tea

【 Ingredients 】

10 g (1/3 oz) fresh mint leaves
80 ml (1/3 C) hot water
10 g (1/3 oz) sheet gelatin
Cold water, as needed
20 g (1 2/3 Tbsp) granulated sugar

5 g (1/8 oz) dry pectin
1 tsp corn syrup
1 tsp lemon juice
Mint for garnish

【 Instructions 】

1. Add mint to a pot and douse with hot water. Steep until strong. Measure out 60 ml (1/4 C) of mint tea.
2. Bloom gelatin in cold water.
3. Combine sugar and pectin.
4. Add mint tea, then sugar and pectin, then corn syrup and lemon juice to a small pan and heat. Once gently boiling, turn heat to low and stir for 2 minutes.

5. Turn off heat. Add well-drained gelatin and stir slowly with spatula, taking care to avoid adding bubbles. Once gelatin is dissolved, pour liquid into molds until halfway filled. Add garnish mint, top off molds with gummy liquid and let set at room temperature.

Rose Hip & Hibiscus Tea

【 Ingredients 】

1 bag rose hip & hibiscus tea
80 ml (1/3 C) hot water
10 g (1/3 oz) sheet gelatin
Cold water, as needed
20 g (1 2/3 Tbsp) granulated sugar

5 g (1/8 oz) dry pectin
1 tsp corn syrup

【 Instructions 】

1. Place tea bag in a pot and douse with hot water. Steep until strong. Measure out 60 ml (1/4 C) of mint tea.
2. Bloom gelatin in cold water.
3. Combine sugar and pectin.
4. Add mint tea, then sugar and pectin, then corn syrup to a small pan and heat. Once gently boiling, turn heat to low and stir for 2 minutes.

5. Turn off heat. Add well-drained gelatin and stir slowly with spatula, taking care to avoid adding bubbles. Once gelatin is dissolved, pour liquid into molds and let set at room temperature.
* Lemon juice is usually added to pectin-based recipes to help set it up, but rose hip and hibiscus tea is acidic so skip it here.
* You can use rose hip tea and hibiscus tea separately for this recipe.

ROSE HIP
&
HIBISCUS TEA

MINT TEA

49

Coffee and Black Tea

Just add milk to coffee or black tea for a crowd-pleasing recipe. Be sure to use skim milk, as full-fat won't keep for very long. With the caramel milk tea, be sure to avoid burning the caramel as that would make it bitter.

Coffee & Milk

[Ingredients]
10 g (2 Tbsp) ground coffee
100 ml (2/5 C) hot water
15 g (1/2 oz) sheet gelatin
Cold water, as needed
30 g (2 1/2 Tbsp) granulated
    sugar
1 tsp corn syrup
5 ml (1 tsp) skim milk

[Instructions]
1. Brew coffee. Measure out 60 ml (1/4 C).
2. Bloom gelatin in cold water.
3. Add coffee, sugar, corn syrup and milk to a small pan (ph.) and heat. Once sugar is dissolved and mixture is gently boiling turn off heat. Add well-drained gelatin.
4. Stir with a spatula, taking care to avoid adding bubbles. Once gelatin is dissolved, pour liquid into molds and let set at room temperature.

Black Tea

[Ingredients]
5 g (appx. 2 bags) Earl Grey tea
100 ml (2/5 C) hot water
15 g (1/2 oz) sheet gelatin
Cold water, as needed
30 g (2 1/2 Tbsp) granulated sugar
1 tsp corn syrup

[Instructions]
Follow instructions for Coffee & Milk gummies. In step 1, steep Earl Grey and measure out 80 ml (1/3 C). Skip skim milk in step 3. The rest is the same.

Caramel Milk Tea

[Ingredients]
5 g (appx. 2 bags) Earl Grey tea
100 ml (2/5 C) hot water
40 g (3 1/4 Tbsp) granulated
    sugar
15 g (1/2 oz) sheet gelatin
Cold water, as needed
1 tsp corn syrup
5 ml (1 tsp) skim milk

[Instructions]
1. Place Earl Grey in a pot and douse with hot water. Steep until strong. Measure out 80 ml (1/3 C).
2. Bloom gelatin in cold water.
3. Add half of sugar (20 g) to a small pan and heat until caramelized (ph.). Turn off heat and add tea (careful, it might spatter). Rock pan to blend tea and sugar.
4. Add remaining sugar, corn syrup and milk to pan and turn on heat. Once sugar has dissolved and mixture is gently boiling, turn off heat and add well-drained gelatin.
5. Stir with a spatula, taking care to avoid adding bubbles. Once gelatin is dissolved, pour liquid into molds and let set at room temperature.

CARAMEL
MILK TEA

COFFEE & MILK

BLACK
TEA

Fun with Gummies

Azuki Beans

Sweet Beans

Chestnuts

Goji Berries

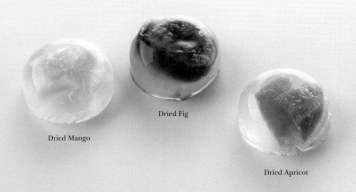

Dried Fig

Dried Mango

Dried Apricot

Chocolate

Gummies with Fillings

Try adding various fillings to gummies from sweet
beans to dried fruits to tiny chocolates. Different
fillings will give different textures to the finished
gummies. These are a treat for the eyes as well as
the palate. Try using unusual ingredients as fillings.

Three-Layer Gummies

Use two kinds of gummy liquid poured in three layers, let set,
then slice with a knife. Try combining vivid red rose hip &
hibiscus tea gummy with white Calpico gummy for a cheerful
treat. Combine Calpico with mint tea for a refined gummy.
Try adding more for four- or five-layer gummies.

Gift Gummies

Gummies that come in charming shapes and colors make for perfect gifts. Here are some wrapping ideas that work well with these tiny goodies.

1. Boxed Gummies
Line a box with colorful gummies. When the recipients open the box, they're sure to say, "Wow, pretty!" Simply place the gummies in small paper cups for a perfect gift.

2. Gummy Necklace
Twist cellophane around individual gummies and tie ends together with ribbon to form a chain. The gummies will glitter like gemstones, and unwrapping each one will be an exciting treat in itself.

3. Gummy Spoons
Place a gummy bear on a wooden spoon, wrap in cellophane and seal with a twist tie. These are perfect for kids' birthdays or as party favors.

4. Gummy Card
Place gummies in a clear plastic bag and staple to a patterned postcard. Add felt or other kinds of decorations. This card will be so cute the recipient might not even want to open it to get to the gummies!

1

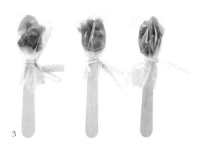

2

3

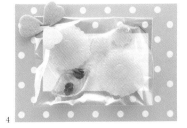

4

Gummy Party

Whip up several types of
gummies and have a gummy
party! They can be eaten by
hand or skewered and dunked
in chocolate fondue, sprinkles,
shredded coconut or crushed
almonds for additional
deliciousness. If you dress
them in melted chocolate,
let stand until solidified.

Aromatic Gummies

Gummies that burst open with a wonderful aroma when eaten add another dimension of excitement. Here I'll introduce gummies made with sweet syrups, liqueurs for adults, ginger and exotic *shiso*. Enjoy the harmony of flavor and color with these gummies.

Aromatic Gummies

I use agar plus gelatin for these gummies. Agar yields a springier texture than gelatin alone.
Agar sets up at room temperature so they're ready in a jiffy. I use sheet gelatin which is more translucent than powdered, allowing the colors of the ingredients to shine through.

【 Basic instructions 】
Strawberry Syrup

1

Bloom sheet gelatin in cold water.

2

Combine sugar and agar.

3

Add syrup and water, then sugar and agar to a small pan.

4

Add corn syrup and lemon juice and heat. If you wet your hands before adding the corn syrup, it won't stick to your finger.

【 Ingredients 】

30 ml (2 Tbsp) strawberry syrup	5 g (1 1/4 tsp) granulated sugar
30 ml (2 Tbsp) water	3 g (1 1/2 tsp) powdered agar
10 g (1/3 oz) sheet gelatin	1 tsp corn syrup
Cold water, as needed	1 tsp lemon juice

5

Stir well with a rubber spatula. Once
agar is dissolved, turn off heat.

6

Wring out gelatin and add to pan.

7

Stir slowly with spatula, taking care
to avoid adding bubbles.

8

Once gelatin is totally dissolved,
pour liquid into molds and let set at
room temperature.

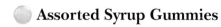 Assorted Syrup Gummies

A wide variety of flavored syrups are available in stores.
They can be used in recipes right out of the bottle and yield vivid, lovely colors. Try making all kinds of syrup gummies!

Blue Curaçao	Passion Fruit	Green Apple	Peach

【 Ingredients and Instructions 】
Follow instructions for Strawberry Syrup gummies (p. 58-59).

STRAWBERRY

PASSION FRUIT   PEACH   BLUE CURAÇAO

GREEN APPLE

🌀 Liqueur Gummies

Liquor-based gummies give off a grown-up mood. The aroma of liqueur that fills your mouth with each bite will please anyone who appreciates spirits. These make perfect presents for men, by the way.

Melon Liqueur   Grand Marnier   Kirsch   Crème de Cassis   Campari

〖 Ingredients and Instructions 〗
Follow instructions for Strawberry Syrup gummies (p. 58-59). Replace syrup with the liqueur of your choice.

Ginger and *Shiso*

You can make gummies out of ingredients that are generally used for garnish or as spice, like ginger and *shiso*. Grate fresh ginger and use the juice squeezed out of the pulp. Boil *shiso* leaves and use the water. Both ingredients have powerful, very Japanese aromas.

Ginger

[Ingredients]

15 ml (1 Tbsp) ginger juice
45 ml (3 Tbsp) water
8 g (1/4 oz) sheet gelatin
Cold water, as needed
30 g (2 1/2 Tbsp) granulated sugar
3 g (1 1/2 tsp) powdered agar
1 tsp corn syrup

[Instructions]

Follow basic instructions for Strawberry Syrup gummies (p. 58-59). In step 3, add ginger juice and water, then sugar and agar to pan (skip lemon juice in step 4). The rest is the same.

Shiso

[Ingredients]

10 leaves *shiso* (or parsley)
70 ml (1/3 C) water
8 g (1/4 oz) sheet gelatin
Cold water, as needed
30 g (2 1/2 Tbsp) granulated sugar
3 g (1 1/2 tsp) powdered agar
1 tsp corn syrup
1 tsp lemon juice

[Instructions]

Follow basic instructions for Strawberry Syrup gummies (p. 58-59). In preparation, bring water to a boil and add 7 *shiso* leaves (ph.). Turn heat to low and simmer for 1 to 2 minutes. Remove *shiso* and measure out 60 ml (1/4 C) *shiso* water. Mince remaining 3 *shiso* leaves. In step 3, add *shiso* water to the pan. In step 8, once gelatin has dissolved, stir in minced *shiso*. Pour gummy liquid into molds and let set at room temperature.

GINGER

SHISO

Pâtes de Fruit: Gummies with a French accent

Pâtes de Fruit are candies made from boiled fruit and sugar. These gummies don't contain gelatin; they're held together with the natural pectin found in the fruit and fortified with sugar. Like jam and confit (foods cooked and preserved in oil or sugar), this style of cooking began in Italy and spread through various regions of France in the beginning of the 16th century. Both King Henry II and Henry IV married daughters of the Medici clan of Italy, who brought with them chefs and pâtissiers. At the time, Rome's influence was waning and France was a rising power, yet Italian culture was still more advanced. In order to give their daughters the comforts of home, the Medicis sent along professionals to ensure continued luxurious living and dining. Their style spread through the country, influencing French cuisine.

This type of dressed-up fruit (fruits déguisés) was very expensive, unattainable by common people. They were also labor-intensive, and a cookbook published in Paris in the 16th century details the toils of the pâtissiers who crafted them.

Nowadays Pâtes de Fruit can be found in French pastry shops across the world. These are a different type of gummy from the traditional German variety, their sweetness smacking of French artisanal craftsmanship.

Japanese Gummies

These gummies are a little different from
their European counterparts.

They use Japanese agar (a.k.a. "kanten") instead
of gelatin, yielding a more toothsome texture.

These gummies have a clean flavor.

Here I'll introduce gummies made with whole
fruit and citrus zest.

Japanese *Kanten* Gummies

Please use the powdered variety for these recipes. Cover the simmering apples with a lid to keep moisture from escaping. Once set up, slice into cubes or long strips or whatever shape you please.

【 Basic instructions 】
Apple

1

Peel apple, chop into eighths and remove seeds and stem. Thinly slice.

2

Add apples, 2 Tbsp water and 10 g sugar to a pot and cover tightly with lid. Simmer over medium-low heat.

3

Stir occasionally with a rubber spatula and simmer until apples are soft. If water has cooked off before the apples are softened, add more.

4

Once the apple mixture has thickened enough that the bottom of the pot remains clear after swiping the spatula across, turn off heat.

【 Ingredients 】

1 apple (200 g (7 oz))

2 Tbsp water

10 g (1 1/4 Tbsp) superfine sugar

150 ml (2/3 C) water

4 g (2 tsp) powdered *kanten*

50 g (6 1/4 Tbsp) superfine sugar

1 Tbsp corn syrup

5

In a separate pot, add *kanten* to 150 ml water.

6

Heat and stir with a rubber spatula. Once gently boiling, continue to stir for another 2 minutes.

7

Add 50 g sugar and corn syrup and stir until dissolved. Remove pan from heat. Stir in apple mixture.

8

Pour into a pan and let set at room temperature. Once set, remove from pan and slice into bite-size pieces.

Japanese-Style Fruit Gummies

Here are recipes for *yuzu* and apricot gummies. Tart, flavorful *yuzu* goes great with the texture of *kanten*.
For the dried apricots, stir constantly and crush them as they cook until they're purée-like.
Try dusting the finished gummies with granulated sugar.

Yuzu

[Ingredients]

1 *yuzu* (150 g (5 1/4 oz))	200 ml (4/5 C) water
Water, as needed	4 g (2 tsp) powdered *kanten*
50 g (6 1/4 Tbsp) superfine sugar	40 g (5 Tbsp) superfine sugar
	1 Tbsp corn syrup

[Instructions]

1. Slice *yuzu* in half. Squeeze out juice. Mix juice with water until you have 150 ml (2/3 C).
2. Remove pulp from *yuzu* and julienne rind, including white part (ph.).
3. Add sliced *yuzu* rind, 50 g sugar and 200 ml water to a pot. Turn on heat and stir occasionally. Once water has reduced to about 1 Tbsp, turn off heat and let cool.
4. In a separate pot, add *kanten* to *yuzu* juice. Turn on heat and stir. Once gently boiling, continue to stir for another 2 minutes.

5. Add 40 g sugar and corn syrup to the second pot. Stir in boiled *yuzu* mixture from step 3. Pour into a pan and let set at room temperature. Once set, remove from pan and slice into bite-size pieces.

Apricot

[Ingredients]

50 g (1 3/4 oz) dried apricots	4 g (2 tsp) powdered *kanten*
400 ml (1 2/3 C) water	40 g (5 Tbsp) superfine sugar
150 ml (2/3 C) water	1 Tbsp corn syrup

[Instructions]

1. Add apricots and 400 ml water to a pot. Turn on heat, stirring and mashing apricots until soft.
2. Once apricots are purée-like and the bottom of the pot stays clean when a spatula is swiped across (ph.), turn off heat.
3. In a separate pot, add *kanten* to 150 ml water. Turn on heat and stir. Once gently boiling, continue to stir for another 2 minutes.

4. Add sugar and syrup to the second pot. Remove from heat. Stir in apricot paste from step 2. Pour into a pan and let set at room temperature. Once set, remove from pan and slice into bite-size pieces.

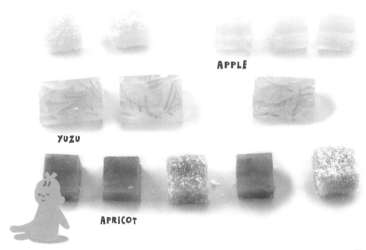

APPLE

YUZU

APRICOT

Hisako Ogita

Born in 1969 in Tokyo, Japan. After graduating with a degree in Sociology from Rikkyo University, Ogita studied for one year at Ecole Tsuji Tokyo. After working for two years at Chandon, a pastry shop in Aoyama, Tokyo, Ogita worked as an assistant to food scientist Yoko Ishihara. She has authored many dessert and pastry cookbooks.

In cooperation with:

Cuoca
http://www.cuoca.com
* Provided ingredients featured in this book

Nut2deco
http://www.nut2deco.com/product-list/144
* Provided plastic models featured in this book

Planning, Composition, Research: Mitsuko Kohashi (Yep)

Art Direction: Yoshie Kawamura (otome-graph.)

Photography: Yasuo Nagumo

Styling: Yuko Magata

Food Prep Assistant: Reiko Takahashi

Illustrations: Ayako Kozen

Editor: Kaori Tanaka

Publisher: Sunao Onuma

Chewy Treats for the Whole Family

Translation: Maya Rosewood

Production: Hiroko Mizuno
             Grace Lu

Vetting: Maria Hostage

Originally published in Japanese as *Jibun de Tsukureru Gumi no Hon* by EDUCATIONAL FOUNDATION BUNKA GAKUEN BUNKA PUBLISHING BUREAU

ISBN: 978-1-935654-90-2

Manufactured in the United States of America

First Edition

Vertical, Inc.
451 Park Avenue South, 7th Floor
New York, NY 10016
www.vertical-inc.com